D0324267

# THE
# STANYAN BOOK
# OF
# CATS

# THE
# STANYAN BOOK
# OF
# CATS

### Edited by
### ALLEN JAMES

STANYAN BOOKS

RANDOM HOUSE

A Stanyan book
Published by Stanyan Books,
8721 Sunset Blvd., Suite C
Hollywood, California 90069,
and by Random House, Inc.
201 East 50th Street,
New York, N.Y. 10022

Library of Congress Catalog
Card Number: 75-149507

Printed in U.S.A.

Designed by Hy Fujita

# PREFACE

What is a cat?

*Felis catus* is a four-legged creature with a furry coat, considerable intelligence, consummate grace and eternal dignity.

He is usually disliked by dog-lovers, who say they do not understand the cat. This is unremarkable because the cat requires a great deal of understanding — including the fact he doesn't give a damn whether you understand him or not.

They prowl with velvet paw through the house, like the *genius loci*, or come and sit down on the table by the writer, keeping his thoughts company, and gazing at him out of the depths of their eyes, dusted with gold, with intelligent tenderness and magical penetration.

**— Théophile Gautier**

# THE RISE OF THE CAT

The cat as we know it today is descended from the civet, a process requiring about ten million years.

Four thousand years ago, the Egyptians revered the cat. To them he was a religious symbol; it was a crime to kill or export a cat.

The form of a cat was given some of the Egyptian gods, notably Pasht, who had the body of a woman but the head of a cat. Not many years ago thousands of mummified cats were found in the temple erected for Pasht. They had been embalmed and buried in mummy cases of fine bronze.

The cat's fertility was very possibly the origin of its worship by the Egyptians. Whatever the reason, the people kept whole armies of cats in the temples, cared for by a special corps of priestesses — and when a sacred cat died, the town went into mourning.

The Egyptians loved their cats so well that when Persians conducting a siege of Pelusium threatened to throw cats over the wall into the city, the Egyptians ran up the white flag.

Some people claim the Chinese were the first to domesticate cats, others bid for citizens of ancient India. Confucius (500 B.C.) was a cat owner, and the cat is mentioned in Sanskrit writings 2000 years old.

In Scandinavia, the Norse goddess Freya was depicted in a chariot drawn by two black cats. The scene became extremely popular, with Freya and her *Felis cati* adopted by hordes of people throughout Western Europe.

The Old Testament did not deign to mention the cat; the reason is believed to be that the Hebrew slaves imported into Egypt grew to loathe the revered cats as well as the Egyptian slave-owners.

The Hebrews' dislike of cats spread northward when Freya's cult was attacked by the Church. Certain prelates announced that worship of Freya was no longer fashionable, and her devotees became subject to torture and death by burning. Freya was branded a witch, and her black companion cats with the golden eyes were deemed messengers of the Devil.

The witch hunt continued well into the 18th century and across the Atlantic; in Salem, Massachusetts, any female suspected of witchery was a sure loser if she owned a cat.

1 35 LEI

Poșta Română

1965                    I. DUMITRANA

# THE COMEBACK OF THE CAT

After millions of cats had been sense-
lessly put to death, reason prevailed and
mankind again looked on *Felis catus*
as a catcher of mice and a decoration on
the hearth, and a friend — when he was in
the mood — to human beings.

The cat was a symbol of victory to the
Romans, of liberty to the Swiss.

In tenth century Britain, the value of a
kitten was a penny (worth a dollar in
those days), and after he captured his
first mouse, twopence. The really good
mousers were priced at fourpence.

The cat is the only creature that will not drink alcoholic beverages. If yours will, please don't write us — just consider him an exceptional cat.

A cat named Brisé fell out of a window when a kitten, and is now so terrified of the great outdoors that she faints the minute she's taken from the house.

A cat cannot see in total darkness.

150 million dollars are spent on cat food each year in the United States.

## DO NOT BRING HOME A CAT IF...

There's a baby in the family. Any cat can be dangerously playful with a helpless infant.

Anyone in the family is allergic to cats.

There's a grown dog in the house. Friendship between adult dogs and cats is possible, but the feat requires time and patience.

40
BANI

Poșta Română

A kitten is more amusing than half the people one is obliged to live with.

— *Lady Sydney Morgan*

The average weight of a newborn kitten is one-quarter pound.

Litters average two to four kittens.

The kitten is blind at birth (Siamese sometimes disproving the fact), and is ten days old before his eyes open.

At birth a kitten has 250 bones — more than a human infant. He has over 500 voluntary muscles which contribute to his acrobatic talents.

A kitten is nursed by his mother until he's about eight weeks old.

The kitten matures in five to eight months, often lives to be 17. The oldest cat on record lived to be 34.

Don't push affection at a kitten. He'll come to you for affection when he's ready for it. He definitely should not be handled a great deal. A kitten is not a toy; he is a baby.

A kitten should always be inoculated for feline enteritis, a deadly contagious disease highly prevalent among cats.

Never shout at a kitten or slap him roughly. He will respond to a tone of voice and, if a bit stubborn, to a gentle whack on his rear with a folded newspaper.

Eight to 12 weeks is the best age for the acquirement of a new kitten. It is wise to first have the kitten thoroughly checked by a veterinarian.

YEMEN ARAB REPUBLIC

1 dh. RAS AL KHAIMA

3 dh. RAS AL KHAIMA

2 dh. RAS AL KHAIMA

YEMEN ½ B

3 Rls. RAS AL KHAIMA

Poșta Română

## SUPERSTITIONS

In the west of England it was believed
that a sore eye would be cured if a cat's
tail were passed over it nine times.

When one hears a cat "singing" at night,
it means that someone in the immediate
area has just gone to his reward.

If a farmer's cat turns his tail
toward the stove or fireplace, his
owner anticipates frost the
following morning.

A black cat is an omen of nasty weather,
according to sailors.

Sailors were horrified by the presence of
a cat aboard their ship, yet it was
believed they would have a safe voyage
if their wives kept a black cat at home.

Rain was indicated if a cat was seen
washing behind its ears with its paws.

In Abyssinian days of yore, any un-
married girl owning a cat was looked on
as a wealthy catch.

المملكة المتوكلية اليمنية

٤ بقش

YEMEN 4 B

## CARE OF THE CAT

A grown cat should be fed one or two meals a day. The latter if he's an eager eater.

Diet:   Aside from commercially prepared cat foods, you can offer from your own larder . . . any raw meat except pork, which must be cooked. Ditto for fish. Milk, of course, and eggs cooked or raw. You can try vegetables, raw or cooked, but always cook and mash potatoes. If your cat turns up his nose, know that he is not a vegetarian.

Catnip is a great idea — until the toy is broken; the stems of the catnip are dangerous for kittens.

If a cat refuses to eat his meal, don't leave the food at his dining place. Put it in the refrigerator and offer it to him at the next mealtime. Don't worry — eventually, he'll eat it. Too many cat owners begin experimenting with different foods and end up serving steak to a fussy eater.

Baths are not recommended, but if a cat gets terribly dirty, perform the operation in a warm room. The bathtub is a good place because the cat can stand with paws on the side. Be sure to plug the ears with cotton. And have everything ready — if you let go for one second, he'll be up on the shower rod. Dry him with a rough towel.

The proper way to pick up a cat . . .
One hand under the hind quarters, the
other under the chest. Never pick him up
by the scruff of the neck — that handling
is reserved for the mother.

## GROOMING

1. Use a broad comb to remove matting.

2. Use a fine-toothed comb to refine the
   process and remove fleas.

3. With a brush, first sweep the fur
   against the line of the coat, then with
   the lie of the fur.

## HOUSEBREAKING

A cat is innately clean, and if a litter
(of shredded newspaper, sand, sawdust,
or a commercial litter) is kept in one
spot, he will soon learn it is his lavatory.

A cat's bed should be placed off the floor, preferably in a quiet corner, as he loathes drafts and loves privacy.

The cat trims his front claws by scratching them on tree trunks. If he is confined indoors, he should be supplied with a scratching post.

The outdoor cat eats grass in order to regurgitate the balls of his own hair — which are inevitable with constant licking. Deprived of grass, the indoor cat's nose should periodically be smeared with petroleum jelly, which acts as a lubricant so that he can pass the hair balls through his intestinal system.

To ascertain a cat's health, look for these points. A glossy coat minus bare spots. Bright eyes. A moist and cool nose. Clean ears. A firm and pink mouth. A respectably clean rear end. A lively personality.

## DISEASES

Face it, the cat is the generator of almost all skin diseases that plague other animals, and man. He is host to worms, fleas, mites and parasites. In addition, he contracts highly contagious diseases such as eczema, trench mouth, tuberculosis, pneumonitis, rhinotracheitis, pseudorabies, plain old rabies —and the most dangerous of all, panleukopenia. The latter is better known as feline enteritis, the virus of which can live unmolested for a year until it finds another cat to infect.

But take heart — and take your cat to a veterinarian as soon as he joins your family. With luck, your pet will escape 99% of these plagues.

المملكة المتوكلية اليمنية

٢ بقش

YEMEN 2B

The cat has a third eyelid, used as protection for the eyeball.

Cat fanciers claim the reason for the M frequently found on the forehead of cats is that Maou was the Egyptian word for cat.

The cat's weight when fully grown averages 10 pounds, his heartbeat is 120 per minute.

Each sex has a disadvantage — the female has her heat periods (endlessly), and the male "sprays." Both problems can be solved by spaying and neutering, respectively.

For those who are helpless in determining the sex of a kitten, here's a simple clue. Lift its tail and *look*. Beneath the tail, the male has a colon (:), the female an exclamation mark,(¡) upside down.

*Homo sapien's* "cat houses" are aptly named, as the *Felis catus* is an incredibly romantic creature. Girl cats are ready for sex at six months, and while boy cats are a year old before they are capable, they make up for lost time. Cat breeders sometimes figure one stud for 30 females.

The 'tomcat fights' for the favors of the queen are silent but vicious, and by the time the tom enters his prime as a stud, at the age of three, he is a scarred veteran. His prowess lasts well through his 14th birthday.

Many females, or queens, are in heat almost constantly if not bred. The female keeps this up well through her eighth year; some queens have produced litters at the ripe age of 25.

The queen announces her condition in a caterwaul that carries unbelievable distances, and all tomcats within earshot respond happily and swiftly.

Occasionally, the *estrus* (heat period) takes place while the cat is pregnant. In such cases it's not uncommon for a cat to give birth to kittens spaced a couple of weeks apart.

A cat queen is a creature who seldom knows the father of her own children. Nor does she care much. The queen will not allow any male near her kittens, as toms are prone to eat their young progeny.

The cat's gestation period is about 62
days. During this time she should be fed
three times a day, with extra calcium,
a dietary procedure that should be main-
tained until the kittens are weaned.

The birthplace:   She will choose it herself — a bureau drawer, the laundry hamper, under the coffee table — unless you provide her with a built-in nest. Line a large box with newspapers and put it in a quiet place — and she'll go to it when her time comes.

The birth:   If the mother cat does not break the sac in which each kitten is born and then cut the umbilical cord — consider yourself a midwife. Cut the cord an inch from the kitten's body and pinch the end to stop any bleeding.

Call the vet if your cat is in labor for more than two hours without giving birth — or if there is no afterbirth (placenta) for each kitten. The latter can cause serious infection.

المملكة المتوكلية اليمنية

١ بقش

YEMEN 1B

Begin weaning kittens when they are
three weeks old with milk food formu-
lated for them commercially. At five
weeks, add scraped raw beef, a spoonful
per feed. After five weeks they should
have four small meals daily: two of milk
with baby cereal added, and two of
either cooked mashed fish, chicken or
beef. At eight weeks when they are fully
weaned, add cow's milk to the cereal
feeds, increasing gradually until they're
ready to go off into their own lives as
drinkers of milk and eaters of meat
and fish.

The cat's tail is his rudder in swimming, his balance whenever his stance is uncertain — and his mood signal. When the tip twitches he's preoccupied, when the tip curls over he's content, when the tail is upright and stiff he couldn't care less about anything, when the tail swishes behind an arched back, beware — and when it merely waves he's in a mood for affection.

The cat does not *need* milk. He does need
protein, and he can do very well without
starch. A cat is not a 'natural eater.' Left
to his own devices he will eat anything,
including things he can't digest, and
even poison.

75 BANI

Poşta Română

1965

I. DUMITRANA

The cat's eyes do not see colors.

Compared to Lassie, the cat is no slouch when it comes to homing instinct. It took the record-breaking cat 18 months, but he *did* travel 1500 miles.

The first formal cat show was held in England in 1871, in America in 1895.

# BREEDS

In general, cats are divided into two breeds — the long and short of it.

*Longhairs* include black, white, blue, cream, blue-cream, tortoiseshell, tortoiseshell-and-white, tabby, brown tabby, red tabby, red self, Peke-faced red, silvery tabby, blue tabby, chinchilla, shaded silver, smoke, red smoke, cameos, Himalayan, Burmese, lilac self, chocolate self, Khmer, Tibetan Temple, Maine Coon Cat, Turkish.

*Shorthairs* include British, American, black, blue-cream, cream, white, British blue, tortoiseshell, tortoiseshell-and-white, tabby, mackerel-striped tabby, spotted, Manx, Siamese, Seal point, blue point, chocolate point, lilac point, tabby point, red point, tortie point, cream point, Russian blue, Abyssinian, Burmese, Havana brown chestnut, Korat, Albino Siamese, Rex.

Following such a list, one breeder deigns to add "Plain or Pet Cat." Inasmuch as this is probably the breed of *your* cat, including yourself in, as Samuel Goldwyn said.

The cat makes over one hundred sounds, each of which has a meaning, at least to other cats. His vocal range includes snarling, spitting, purring, hissing, screaming, growling, trilling, and the famous meow.

Even the purr has its own vocabulary. Anxiety is shown by a sharp purr, pain by a deep purr, contentment by a soft purr.

People who argue about the relative merits of the cat and dog might as well compare a vegetable with a table. The two animals are distinctly different creatures; while the dog has learned to live with man, the cat has not changed over the centuries. A cat is and always will be aloof and independent.

SHQIPERIA 80 q.

mace persiane

The Persian is the most popular of the longhairs, and more sedate than any other breed.

The Abyssinian closely resembles the sacred cat of ancient Egypt. It is gentle and affectionate, and an excellent swimmer.

The Siamese is the best conversationalist, in a voice with a very high pitch.

The Burmese trains well to the leash, is considered by many to be the most dog-like cat.

The formal name of the alley cat is the American Shorthair.

The Manx has no tail and tends to walk with a sort of crouch and hop.

The Russian Blue has less curiosity than other breeds. It is quiet and gentle.

The Persian and the Angora were cross-bred; the Persian dominated to the point that the true Angora is almost non-existent.

The "tabby" cat, with lines and mark-ings in its fur, is so called after the Attabbiah district of Baghdad, where a ribbed silk fabric was woven.

55 BANI

Poșta Română

I. DUMITRANA

When in an affectionate mood, cats have
been known to pat a master's cheek, put
their paws around his neck, or stand on
hindfeet, clawing the air for attention.
Cats can open windows, turn handles,
open refrigerator doors — and one on
record taught himself to somersault by
watching a dog perform.

It is a rare cat that suffers from motion sickness; this goes for automobile and boat trips. Science attributes this to his inner ear — yet his balance is not all it's cracked up to be; the cat does *not* always land on his feet.

Deafness is most common among the
white cats with blue eyes. Remarkable
compensation for deafness results in the
fact that deaf cats are more intelligent.

The whiskers are responsible for the
myth that a cat can see at night.
As sensory organs, they constitute
a flawless radar system.

When I play with my cat, who knows but that she regards me as a plaything even more than I do her?

— *Montaigne*

Cats know how to obtain food without labor, shelter without confinement, and love without penalties.

— *W. L. George*

The cat may look at a King, they say, but rather would look at a mouse at play.

— *Arthur Guiterman,* **A Poet's Proverbs**

The cat is the only non-gregarious domestic animal. It is retained by its extraordinary adhesion to the comforts of the house in which it is reared.

— *Francis Galton*

I have never known a cat that couldn't quiet me down just by walking slowly past my chair.

— **Rod McKuen**

It has been the providence of nature to give this creature nine lives.

— *Pilpay* — Fable III